POWER ROUTINES II

A 30 Day Guided Tour of the
Habits of Gratitude, Scripture Reading, Journaling and Prayer

By Chuck Allen
AChuckAllen.com
@AChuckAllen

POWER ROUTINES II
A 30 Day Guided Tour of the
Habits of Gratitude, Scripture Reading, Journaling and Prayer

Copyright © Sugar Hill Resources
2019 by Chuck Allen

Cover design and layout by
Ethan Hyma
ethan@sugarhillchurch.com

Welcome to Power Routines

For years, I have been captivated by the power discovered in four disciplines that have radically changed my attitudes, energy, and natural emotional swings. Those four disciplines are:

1. **Practicing Intentional Gratitude**
2. **Consistent Scripture Reading**
3. **Mindful and Spiritual Journaling**
4. **Guided Prayer & Meditation**

With much effort, I've searched for a resource that could meet all four of these needs. I also wanted a resource that would assist me in building and sustaining a spiritual habit. After finding no such tool, I set off on the effort to build a tool for myself andbegan to have folks say, "why don't you create your own journal?'"

Knowing that I needed spiritual disciplines in my life caused me to create a simple, yet powerful routine that incorporated these four disciplines. I trust that you will find power in this new habit.

So, here it is, **POWER ROUTINES JOURNAL II**! A guided journey that will take you into thirty days of GRATITUDE, SCRIPTURE READING, JOURNALING, and GUIDED PRAYER.

There is no magic to using this resource, but there is something powerful about developing spiritual habits that solidify your faith, secure you to Christ, and encourage you in the journey of becoming your very best you!

I encourage you to share a copy of Power Routines withsomeone close to you and hold each other accountable to invest just fifteen minutes each day in discovering power in your daily lives!

The reason that I've chosen these five disciplines is simple.

- **Gratitude** is a powerful emotion that can set the course for your day. It dares your attitudes to reflect on the glass half full and the best in life. When I realized that starting my day with gratitude made every single day better, it became an essential part of my days becoming more pleasant, productive, fulfilling, and happy. I am confident that the same will be true for you!

- **Scripture** is at the heart of Power Routines. Of all the books on leadership, life and love, the Holy Scriptures are far beyond them all put together. Years ago, I was challenged to stop investing my time in memorizing Scripture and instead, read Scripture with one desire - TO KNOW GOD MORE FULLY. I now read the Bible each day, not with a desire to check off a task list or hurry through it to prove that I read it. I read Scripture with an intentional desire for it to get inside my heart and my head and transform me into the person and leader God desires me to be. If we are to have a "renewing of our mind," we must invest in saturating our mind with God's Word.

- **Journaling** is simple for some, but a challenge for most. To stare at an empty page and ponder what to write upon it can be a daunting task. That's why Power Routines asks you four simple questions. So, just answer the questions! It will improve your awareness, creativity, and relationships. The key to journaling is to write whatever the truth to the answer is. It is for you, not for public display.

- **Guided Prayer and Meditation** is exactly as it sounds. Building this discipline into your life will absolutely draw you into a closer relationship with the Divine. This is the one Power Routine that also includes an audio sibling (weekdaymeditation.com). First, list *who* you are praying for and why. Then, list *what* you are praying for. Next, list answers to prayers that you see, experience, and believe. Once done, listen to the WeekdayMeditation.com, and let me walk you through a guided prayer and a short time of quietude and solitude each day.

I know that you are incredibly busy, but when I made time for Power Routines, I found a far better way to live. It is worth dropping a few existing habits and adding a power-packed habit in its place.

The number one question that I am asked about Power Routines is this: "How do you practically do this every day?" My answer? Start small, dream big, and trust God. Here is my typical morning routine:

- Gratitude: What three things am I grateful for? (2 minutes)
- Read Scripture: (5 minutes)
- Journal: Answer the five questions. (3 minutes)
- Pray and Meditate: This includes listening and praying with the Weekday Meditation. (10 minutes)

If you were keeping track, that's about twenty minutes. You can probably accomplish all of this in fifteen minutes, if you prefer. It's not a race; it's a habit. Habits are best created when we start small and add as we find benefit. I have no doubt that you will find great benefit from developing these four **POWER ROUTINES!**

The Simple Journey to POWER Starts With
The Most Simple PLAN

If you are like me, I am so grateful for GPS in my truck. My brain can get distracted much faster than my ability to focus on where I am or where I am going. That's why I love to use Waze as my guidance system. I can tell Waze where I wish to go and in the voice of a boy band it will tell me melodically, "turn right... then turn left." Power Routines is just that simple. Each day for the next thirty days, I'll walk you through four daily spiritual disciplines:

- **GRATITUDE:** Start each day with one question. What three things are you grateful for today? Then simply answer in the space provided. I have discovered the life-altering power of daily gratitude. Nothing has changed my life quite like starting every single day with an attitude of gratitude.

- **SCRIPTURE:** There is overwhelming power and peace to be experienced when we intentionally take God's Word and let it sink deep into our souls. Nothing can give us hope, wisdom, and conviction like getting the Scriptures into our heads and hearts.

- **JOURNALING:** Don't be intimidated by journaling. Journaling is answering simple questions. You might answer with one word or fifty words, but the key is to think deeply and spontaneously enough to capture what is stirring in your heart, mind, and soul at that moment.

- **PRAYER:** I want to simplify your prayer life by giving you a few prayer prompts to launch your conversations with the Divine. This prayer routine can be repeated over and over throughout your day. For most of you, I want to eliminate your guilt about the amount of time you spend in daily prayer and help you experience a time of significant prayer. Add the Weekday Meditation to this Power Routine and watch how the Lord speaks into your life!

That seems simple enough, right? Less than twenty minutes each day and you can build a spiritual POWER ROUTINE into your life!

Let's Do This!

Chuck Allen

SAMPLE

1. *A good nights sleep*
2. *Payday is today*
3. *My family is healthy*

When you are grateful for what you have, what you have is more than enough.

SCRIPTURE
Proverbs

Proverbs 1:32-33
For simpletons turn away from me—to death. Fools are destroyed by their own complacency. But all who listen to me will live in peace, untroubled by fear of harm.

SCRIPTURE
Old Testament

Joshua 1:6-8
Be strong and very courageous. Be careful to obey all the instructions Moses gave you. Do not deviate from them, turning either to the right or to the left. Then you will be successful in everything you do. Study this Book of Instruction continually. Meditate on it day and night so you will be sure to obey everything written in it. Only then will you prosper and succeed in all you do.

SCRIPTURE
New Testament

Hebrews 10:24-25
Let us think of ways to motivate one another to acts of love and good works. And let us not neglect our meeting together, as some people do, but encourage one another, especially now that the day of his return is drawing near.

1. What is the Lord speaking into your life through these verses?

Listening to God allows me to have peace in my life, and if I obey his commands, He will allow me to be successful.

2. What did you learn about the Lord?

The Lord is peace and He will allow me to succeed.

Yesterday's Wins: _My work presentation went well!_

Yesterday's Challenges: _It was hard for me to get out of bed._

Lessons Learned: _I need to listen more and talk less._

Today's Declaration: Today, I will...

Get my work done and get to spend time with family.

Who? _Barbra_   Why? _Cancer_

Who? _Mark_   Why? _Tough Divorce_

Who? _Lisa_   Why? _Finances_

What? _That John does well in his new job._

What? _____

Praise: _Thank you Jesus for my health._

Answered Prayers: _Mike has recovered from his surgery._
My uncle was able to sell his house.

> Prayer's important, not just as some kind
> of a metaphysical exercise, but I think it's a
> way to refresh one's own mind and motive.
> -Mike Huckabee

> You're going to go through tough times - that's life. But I say, 'Nothing happens to you, it happens for you.' See the positive in negative events.
> -Joel Osteen

ADDITIONAL THOUGHTS

Jesus is all that I need in my life.
I will have bad days but He will always be by
my side.

Discover Peace, Power, & Direction
ON THE WEEKDAY MEDITATION
Meditative prayer guided by Pastor Chuck Allen
WeekdayMeditation.com

WEEKDAY
MEDITATION

GRATITUDE
Today, I am grateful for...

1. _____

2. _____

3. _____

When you are grateful for what you have, what you have is more than enough.

SCRIPTURE
Proverbs

Proverbs 1:22-23
How long, you simpletons, will you insist on being simpleminded? How long will you mockers relish your mocking? How long will you fools hate knowledge? Come and listen to my counsel. I'll share my heart with you and make you wise.

SCRIPTURE
Old Testament

Deuteronomy 6:4-6
Listen, O Israel! The Lord is our God, the Lord alone. And you must love the Lord your God with all your heart, all your soul, and all your strength. And you must commit yourselves wholeheartedly to these commands that I am giving you today.

SCRIPTURE
New Testament

1 Timothy 4:8-10
Physical training is good, but training for godliness is much better, promising benefits in this life and in the life to come. This is a trustworthy saying, and everyone should accept it. This is why we work hard and continue to struggle, for our hope is in the living God.

1. What is the Lord speaking into your life through these verses?

_____

_____

_____

2. What did you learn about the Lord?

_____

_____

Yesterday's Wins: _____

Yesterday's Challenges: _____

Lessons Learned: _____

_____

Today's Declaration: Today, I will...

_____

Who? _____ Why? _____

Who? _____ Why? _____

Who? _____ Why? _____

What? _____

What? _____

Praise: _____

Answered Prayers: _____

_____

_____

> I pray to start my day and finish it in prayer. I'm just
> thankful for everything, all the blessings in my life,
> trying to stay that way.
> -Tim Tebow

> I believe in Christianity as I believe that the sun has risen: not only because I see it, but because by it I see everything else.
> -C.S. Lewis

ADDITIONAL THOUGHTS

_____

_____

_____

_____

_____

_____

_____

_____

_____

_____

**WANT TO FILL YOUR DAY WITH
A CUP OF ENCOURAGEMENT?**
Experience the Weekday Podcast | *WeekdayPodcast.com*
5 minutes a day and 5 days a week
WeekdayPodcast.com

GRATITUDE
Today, I am grateful for...

1. _____

2. _____

3. _____

When you are grateful for what you have, what you have is more than enough.

Proverbs 1:32-33
*For simpletons turn away from me—to death. Fools
are destroyed by their own complacency. But all who
listen to me will live in peace, untroubled by fear of
harm.*

SCRIPTURE
Proverbs

Joshua 1:6-8
*Be strong and very courageous. Be careful to obey all
the instructions Moses gave you. Do not deviate from
them, turning either to the right or to the left. Then you
will be successful in everything you do. Study this Book
of Instruction continually. Meditate on it day and night
so you will be sure to obey everything written in it.
Only then will you prosper and succeed in all you do.*

SCRIPTURE
Old Testament

Hebrews 10:24-25
*Let us think of ways to motivate one another to acts
of love and good works. And let us not neglect our
meeting together, as some people do, but encourage
one another, especially now that the day of his return
is drawing near.*

SCRIPTURE
New Testament

1. What is the Lord speaking into your life through these verses?

_____

_____

_____

2. What did you learn about the Lord?

_____

_____

Yesterday's Wins: _____

Yesterday's Challenges: _____

Lessons Learned: _____

_____

Today's Declaration: Today, I will...

_____

PRAYER
Today, I am praying for...

Who? _____   Why? _____

Who? _____   Why? _____

Who? _____   Why? _____

What? _____

What? _____

Praise: _____

Answered Prayers: _____

_____

_____

> Prayer's important, not just as some kind
> of a metaphysical exercise, but I think it's a
> way to refresh one's own mind and motive.
> -Mike Huckabee

> You're going to go through tough times -
> that's life. But I say, 'Nothing happens to
> you, it happens for you.' See the positive
> in negative events.
> -Joel Osteen

ADDITIONAL THOUGHTS

_____

_____

_____

_____

_____

_____

_____

_____

_____

_____

Discover Peace, Power, & Direction
ON THE WEEKDAY MEDITATION
Meditative prayer guided by Pastor Chuck Allen
WeekdayMeditation.com

WEEKDAY
MEDITATION

POWER ROUTINES _____ • _____ • _____   S   M   T   W   TH   F   S

GRATITUDE
Today, I am grateful for...

1. _____

2. _____

3. _____

When you are grateful for what you have, what you have is more than enough.

SCRIPTURE
Proverbs

Proverbs 2:1-3
My child, listen to what I say, and treasure my commands. Tune your ears to wisdom, and concentrate on understanding. Cry out for insight, and ask for understanding.

SCRIPTURE
Old Testament

Psalm 3:3-4
But you, O Lord, are a shield around me; you are my glory, the one who holds my head high. I cried out to the Lord, and he answered me from his holy mountain.

SCRIPTURE
New Testament

John 15:1-3
I am the true grapevine, and my Father is the gardener. He cuts off every branch of mine that doesn't produce fruit, and he prunes the branches that do bear fruit so they will produce even more. You have already been pruned and purified by the message I have given you.

1. What is the Lord speaking into your life through these verses?

_____

_____

_____

2. What did you learn about the Lord?

_____

_____

Yesterday's Wins: _____

Yesterday's Challenges: _____

Lessons Learned: _____

_____

Today's Declaration: Today, I will...

_____

PRAYER
Today, I am praying for...

Who? _____ Why? _____

Who? _____ Why? _____

Who? _____ Why? _____

What? _____

What? _____

Praise: _____

Answered Prayers: _____

_____

_____

Spend more time in study and prayer.
That's the secret of successful evangelism.
-Billy Graham

> The best and most beautiful things
> in this world cannot be seen or even
> heard, but must be felt with the heart.
> -Helen Keller

ADDITIONAL THOUGHTS

_____

_____

_____

_____

_____

_____

_____

_____

_____

_____

**WANT TO FILL YOUR DAY WITH
A CUP OF ENCOURAGEMENT?**
Experience the Weekday Podcast | _WeekdayPodcast.com_
5 minutes a day and 5 days a week
WeekdayPodcast.com

1. _____

2. _____

3. _____

When you are grateful for what you have, what you have is more than enough.

Proverbs 2:20-22
So follow the steps of the good, and stay on the paths of the righteous. For only the godly will live in the land, and those with integrity will remain in it. But the wicked will be removed from the land, and the treacherous will be uprooted.

SCRIPTURE
Proverbs

Deuteronomy 31:5-6
The Lord will hand over to you the people who live there, and you must deal with them as I have commanded you. So be strong and courageous! Do not be afraid and do not panic before them. For the Lord your God will personally go ahead of you. He will neither fail you nor abandon you.

SCRIPTURE
Old Testament

Acts 2:17-19
God says, 'I will pour out my Spirit upon all people. Your sons and daughters will prophesy. Your young men will see visions, and your old men will dream dreams. In those days I will pour out my Spirit even on my servants—men and women alike— and they will prophesy. And I will cause wonders in the heavens.

SCRIPTURE
New Testament

1. What is the Lord speaking into your life through these verses?

_____

_____

_____

2. What did you learn about the Lord?

_____

_____

Yesterday's Wins: _____

Yesterday's Challenges: _____

Lessons Learned: _____

_____

Today's Declaration: Today, I will...

_____

Who? _____   Why? _____

Who? _____   Why? _____

Who? _____   Why? _____

What? _____

What? _____

Praise: _____

Answered Prayers: _____

_____

_____

Prayer is as natural an expression of faith as
breathing is of life.
-Jonathan Edwards

Life is like riding a bicycle. To keep your
balance, you must keep moving.
-Albert Einstein

ADDITIONAL THOUGHTS

_____

_____

_____

_____

_____

_____

_____

_____

_____

_____

_____

Discover Peace, Power, & Direction
ON THE WEEKDAY MEDITATION
Meditative prayer guided by Pastor Chuck Allen
WeekdayMeditation.com

WEEKDAY
MEDITATION

GRATITUDE
Today, I am grateful for...

1. _____

2. _____

3. _____

When you are grateful for what you have, what you have is more than enough.

SCRIPTURE
Proverbs

Proverbs 3:1-3
My child, never forget the things I have taught you. Store my commands in your heart. If you do this, you will live many years, and your life will be satisfying. Never let loyalty and kindness leave you! Tie them around your neck as a reminder. Write them deep within your heart.

SCRIPTURE
Old Testament

Genesis 1:1-2
In the beginning God created the heavens and the earth. The earth was formless and empty, and darkness covered the deep waters. And the Spirit of God was hovering over the surface of the waters.

SCRIPTURE
New Testament

1 Corinthians 7:21-23
Are you a slave? Don't let that worry you—but if you get a chance to be free, take it. And remember, if you were a slave when the Lord called you, you are now free in the Lord. And if you were free when the Lord called you, you are now a slave of Christ. God paid a high price for you, so don't be enslaved by the world.

1. What is the Lord speaking into your life through these verses?

_____

_____

_____

2. What did you learn about the Lord?

_____

_____

Yesterday's Wins: _____

Yesterday's Challenges: _____

Lessons Learned: _____

_____

Today's Declaration: Today, I will...

_____

PRAYER
Today, I am praying for...

Who? _____ Why? _____

Who? _____ Why? _____

Who? _____ Why? _____

What? _____

What? _____

Praise: _____

Answered Prayers: _____

_____

_____

Prayer in private results
in boldness in public.
-Edwin Louis Cole

> Each life is made up of mistakes and learning,
> waiting and growing, practicing
> patience and being persistent.
> -Billy Graham

ADDITIONAL THOUGHTS

_____

_____

_____

_____

_____

_____

_____

_____

_____

_____

_____

**WANT TO FILL YOUR DAY WITH
A CUP OF ENCOURAGEMENT?**
Experience the Weekday Podcast | _WeekdayPodcast.com_
5 minutes a day and 5 days a week
WeekdayPodcast.com

POWER ROUTINES _____ • _____ • _____   S M T W TH F S

1. _____

2. _____

3. _____

When you are grateful for what you have, what you have is more than enough.

Proverbs 3:11-12
My child, don't reject the Lord 's discipline, and don't be upset when he corrects you. For the Lord corrects those he loves, just as a father corrects a child in whom he delights.

SCRIPTURE
Proverbs

Ecclesiastes 2:25-26
For who can eat or enjoy anything apart from him? God gives wisdom, knowledge, and joy to those who please him. But if a sinner becomes wealthy, God takes the wealth away and gives it to those who please him. This, too, is meaningless—like chasing the wind.

SCRIPTURE
Old Testament

Romans 5:3-4
We can rejoice, too, when we run into problems and trials, for we know that they help us develop endurance. And endurance develops strength of character, and character strengthens our confident hope of salvation.

SCRIPTURE
New Testament

1. What is the Lord speaking into your life through these verses?

_____

_____

_____

2. What did you learn about the Lord?

_____

_____

27

Yesterday's Wins: _____

Yesterday's Challenges: _____

Lessons Learned: _____

_____

Today's Declaration: Today, I will...

_____

PRAYER
Today, I am praying for...

Who? _____   Why? _____

Who? _____   Why? _____

Who? _____   Why? _____

What? _____

What? _____

Praise: _____

Answered Prayers: _____

_____

_____

The sovereign cure for worry is prayer.
-William James

> Our greatest happiness does not depend on the condition of life in which chance has placed us, but is always the result of a good conscience, good health, occupation and freedom in all just pursuits.
> -Thomas Jefferson

ADDITIONAL THOUGHTS

_____

_____

_____

_____

_____

_____

_____

_____

_____

_____

_____

Discover Peace, Power, & Direction
ON THE WEEKDAY MEDITATION
Meditative prayer guided by Pastor Chuck Allen
WeekdayMeditation.com

WEEKDAY
MEDITATION

POWER ROUTINES _____ • _____ • _____   S M T W TH F S

GRATITUDE
Today, I am grateful for...

1. _____

2. _____

3. _____

When you are grateful for what you have, what you have is more than enough.

SCRIPTURE
Proverbs

Proverbs 4:4-6
My father taught me, "Take my words to heart. Follow my commands, and you will live. Get wisdom; develop good judgment. Don't forget my words or turn away from them. Don't turn your back on wisdom, for she will protect you. Love her, and she will guard you.

SCRIPTURE
Old Testament

1 Samuel 12:20-22
"Don't be afraid," Samuel reassured them. "You have certainly done wrong, but make sure now that you worship the Lord with all your heart, and don't turn your back on him. Don't go back to worshiping worthless idols that cannot help or rescue you—they are totally useless! The Lord will not abandon his people, because that would dishonor his great name."

SCRIPTURE
New Testament

Matthew 3:11-12
I baptize with water those who repent of their sins and turn to God. But someone is coming soon who is greater than I am—so much greater that I'm not worthy even to be his slave and carry his sandals. He will baptize you with the Holy Spirit and with fire. He is ready to separate the chaff from the wheat...

1. What is the Lord speaking into your life through these verses?

_____

_____

_____

2. What did you learn about the Lord?

_____

_____

Yesterday's Wins: _____

Yesterday's Challenges: _____

Lessons Learned: _____

_____

Today's Declaration: Today, I will...

_____

Who? _____ Why? _____

Who? _____ Why? _____

Who? _____ Why? _____

What? _____

What? _____

Praise: _____

Answered Prayers: _____

_____

_____

In our home there was always prayer -
aloud, proud and unapologetic.
-Lyndon B. Johnson

31

> The time you spend alone with God will transform your character and increase your devotion. Then yourintegrity and god behavior in an unbelieving world will make other long to know the Lord.
> -Charles Stanley

ADDITIONAL THOUGHTS

_____

_____

_____

_____

_____

_____

_____

_____

_____

_____

**WANT TO FILL YOUR DAY WITH
A CUP OF ENCOURAGEMENT?**
Experience the Weekday Podcast | *WeekdayPodcast.com*
5 minutes a day and 5 days a week
WeekdayPodcast.com

POWER ROUTINES _____ • _____ • _____   S M T W TH F S

GRATITUDE
Today, I am grateful for...

1. _____

2. _____

3. _____

When you are grateful for what you have, what you have is more than enough.

SCRIPTURE
Proverbs

Proverbs 4:25-27
Look straight ahead, and fix your eyes on what lies before you. Mark out a straight path for your feet; stay on the safe path. Don't get sidetracked; keep your feet from following evil.

SCRIPTURE
Old Testament

2 Samuel 7:21-22
Because of your promise and according to your will, you have done all these great things and have made them known to your servant. "How great you are, O Sovereign Lord! There is no one like you. We have never even heard of another God like you!"

SCRIPTURE
New Testament

Matthew 4:2-4
For forty days and forty nights he fasted and became very hungry. During that time the devil came and said to him, "If you are the Son of God, tell these stones to become loaves of bread." But Jesus told him, "No! The Scriptures say, 'People do not live by bread alone, but by every word that comes from the mouth of God.'"

1. What is the Lord speaking into your life through these verses?

_____

_____

_____

2. What did you learn about the Lord?

_____

_____

Yesterday's Wins: _____

Yesterday's Challenges: _____

Lessons Learned: _____

_____

Today's Declaration: Today, I will...

_____

Who? _____   Why? _____

Who? _____   Why? _____

Who? _____   Why? _____

What? _____

What? _____

Praise: _____

Answered Prayers: _____

_____

_____

Amen is not the end of a prayer, it just gets
us ready to go to the next level.
-Gary Busey

> With the new day comes new strength
> and new thoughts.
> -Eleanor Roosevelt

ADDITIONAL THOUGHTS

_____

_____

_____

_____

_____

_____

_____

_____

_____

_____

Discover Peace, Power, & Direction
ON THE WEEKDAY MEDITATION
Meditative prayer guided by Pastor Chuck Allen
WeekdayMeditation.com

WEEKDAY
MEDITATION

GRATITUDE
Today, I am grateful for...

1. _____

2. _____

3. _____

When you are grateful for what you have, what you have is more than enough.

SCRIPTURE
Proverbs

Proverbs 6:12-14
What are worthless and wicked people like? They are constant liars, signaling their deceit with a wink of the eye, a nudge of the foot, or the wiggle of fingers. Their perverted hearts plot evil, and they constantly stir up trouble.

SCRIPTURE
Old Testament

Psalm 23:1-3
The Lord is my shepherd; I have all that I need. He lets me rest in green meadows; he leads me beside peaceful streams. He renews my strength. He guides me along right paths, bringing honor to his name.

SCRIPTURE
New Testament

Matthew 5:3-5
God blesses those who are poor and realize their need for him, Greek poor in spirit. for the Kingdom of Heaven is theirs. God blesses those who mourn, for they will be comforted. God blesses those who are humble, for they will inherit the whole earth.

1. What is the Lord speaking into your life through these verses?

_____

_____

_____

2. What did you learn about the Lord?

_____

_____

Yesterday's Wins: _____

Yesterday's Challenges: _____

Lessons Learned: _____

_____

Today's Declaration: Today, I will...

_____

PRAYER
Today, I am praying for...

Who? _____ Why? _____

Who? _____ Why? _____

Who? _____ Why? _____

What? _____

What? _____

Praise: _____

Answered Prayers: _____

_____

_____

Today I think that prayer is just simply a necessity,
because by prayer I believe we mean an effort to
get in touch with the Infinite.
-Dwight D. Eisenhower

> To me, every hour of the day and night is an
> unspeakably perfect miracle.
> -Walt Whitman

ADDITIONAL THOUGHTS

_____

_____

_____

_____

_____

_____

_____

_____

_____

_____

**WANT TO FILL YOUR DAY WITH
A CUP OF ENCOURAGEMENT?**
Experience the Weekday Podcast | *WeekdayPodcast.com*
5 minutes a day and 5 days a week
WeekdayPodcast.com

POWER ROUTINES _____ • _____ • _____   S M T W TH F S

1. _____

2. _____

3. _____

When you are grateful for what you have, what you have is more than enough.

Proverbs 6:30-31
Excuses might be found for a thief who steals because he is starving. But if he is caught, he must pay back seven times what he stole, even if he has to sell everything in his house.

SCRIPTURE
Proverbs

Psalm 150:1-3
Praise the Lord! Praise God in his sanctuary; praise him in his mighty heaven! Praise him for his mighty works; praise his unequaled greatness! Praise him with a blast of the ram's horn; praise him with the lyre and harp!

SCRIPTURE
Old Testament

Mark 1:16-18
One day as Jesus was walking along the shore of the Sea of Galilee, he saw Simon and his brother Andrew throwing a net into the water, for they fished for a living. Jesus called out to them, "Come, follow me, and I will show you how to fish for people!" And they left their nets at once and followed him.

SCRIPTURE
New Testament

1. What is the Lord speaking into your life through these verses?

_____

_____

_____

2. What did you learn about the Lord?

_____

_____

Yesterday's Wins: _____

Yesterday's Challenges: _____

Lessons Learned: _____

_____

Today's Declaration: Today, I will...

_____

PRAYER
Today, I am praying for...

Who? _____   Why? _____

Who? _____   Why? _____

Who? _____   Why? _____

What? _____

What? _____

Praise: _____

Answered Prayers: _____

_____

_____

All of us should not attempt to fulfill the
responsibilities we now have without prayer
and a strong faith in God.
-George H.W. Bush

> As we express our gratitude, we must never forget that the highest appreciation is not to utter words, but to live by them.
> -John F. Kennedy

ADDITIONAL THOUGHTS

_____

_____

_____

_____

_____

_____

_____

_____

_____

_____

Discover Peace, Power, & Direction
ON THE WEEKDAY MEDITATION
Meditative prayer guided by Pastor Chuck Allen
WeekdayMeditation.com

WEEKDAY
MEDITATION

GRATITUDE
Today, I am grateful for...

1. _____

2. _____

3. _____

When you are grateful for what you have, what you have is more than enough.

SCRIPTURE
Proverbs

Proverbs 8:13-14
All who fear the Lord will hate evil. Therefore, I hate pride and arrogance, corruption and perverse speech. Common sense and success belong to me. Insight and strength are mine.

SCRIPTURE
Old Testament

Psalm 23:1-3
O Lord , I will honor and praise your name, for you are my God. You do such wonderful things! You planned them long ago, and now you have accomplished them. You turn mighty cities into heaps of ruins. Cities with strong walls are turned to rubble. Beautiful palaces in distant lands disappear and will never be rebuilt. Strong nations will declare your glory.

SCRIPTURE
New Testament

Luke 7:22-23
Then he told John's disciples, "Go back to John and tell him what you have seen and heard—the blind see, the lame walk, those with leprosy are cured, the deaf hear, the dead are raised to life, and the Good News is being preached to the poor." And he added, "God blesses those who do not fall away because of me."

1. What is the Lord speaking into your life through these verses?

_____

_____

_____

2. What did you learn about the Lord?

_____

_____

Yesterday's Wins: _____

Yesterday's Challenges: _____

Lessons Learned: _____

_____

Today's Declaration: Today, I will...

_____

PRAYER
Today, I am praying for...

Who? _____ Why? _____

Who? _____ Why? _____

Who? _____ Why? _____

What? _____

What? _____

Praise: _____

Answered Prayers: _____

_____

_____

Time spent in prayer is never wasted.
-Francois Fenelon

> We are saved by faith alone, but the faith that saves is never alone.
> -Martin Luther

ADDITIONAL THOUGHTS

_____

_____

_____

_____

_____

_____

_____

_____

_____

_____

THE WEEKDAY PODCAST

**WANT TO FILL YOUR DAY WITH
A CUP OF ENCOURAGEMENT?**
Experience the Weekday Podcast | _WeekdayPodcast.com_
5 minutes a day and 5 days a week
WeekdayPodcast.com

POWER ROUTINES _____ • _____ • _____   S M T W TH F S

GRATITUDE
Today, I am grateful for...

1. _____

2. _____

3. _____

When you are grateful for what you have, what you have is more than enough.

Proverbs 8:17-19
I love all who love me. Those who search will surely find me. I have riches and honor, as well as enduring wealth and justice. My gifts are better than gold, even the purest gold, my wages better than sterling silver!

SCRIPTURE
Proverbs

Leviticus 5:5-6
When you become aware of your guilt in any of these ways, you must confess your sin. Then you must bring to the Lord as the penalty for your sin a female from the flock, either a sheep or a goat. This is a sin offering with which the priest will purify you from your sin, making you right with the Lord.

SCRIPTURE
Old Testament

2 Corinthians 3:16-18
But whenever someone turns to the Lord, the veil is taken away. For the Lord is the Spirit, and wherever the Spirit of the Lord is, there is freedom. So all of us who have had that veil removed can see and reflect the glory of the Lord. And the Lord, who is the Spirit- makes us more and more like him as we are changed.

SCRIPTURE
New Testament

1. What is the Lord speaking into your life through these verses?

_____

_____

_____

2. What did you learn about the Lord?

_____

_____

45

Yesterday's Wins: _____

Yesterday's Challenges: _____

Lessons Learned: _____

_____

Today's Declaration: Today, I will...

_____

Who? _____   Why? _____

Who? _____   Why? _____

Who? _____   Why? _____

What? _____

What? _____

Praise: _____

Answered Prayers: _____

_____

_____

Prayer is the Key to heaven but faith unlocks the door.
-Anonymous

> Be strong and courageous. Do not be afraid or terrified because of them, for the LORD your God goes with you; he will never leave you nor forsake you.
> -Deuteronomy 31:6

ADDITIONAL THOUGHTS

_____

_____

_____

_____

_____

_____

_____

_____

_____

_____

_____

Discover Peace, Power, & Direction
ON THE WEEKDAY MEDITATION
Meditative prayer guided by Pastor Chuck Allen
WeekdayMeditation.com

WEEKDAY
MEDITATION

GRATITUDE
Today, I am grateful for...

1. _____

2. _____

3. _____

When you are grateful for what you have, what you have is more than enough.

SCRIPTURE
Proverbs

Proverbs 8:34-36
Joyful are those who listen to me, watching for me daily at my gates, waiting for me outside my home! For whoever finds me finds life and receives favor from the Lord . But those who miss me injure themselves. All who hate me love death.

SCRIPTURE
Old Testament

Exodus 19:5-6
Now if you will obey me and keep my covenant, you will be my own special treasure from among all the peoples on earth; for all the earth belongs to me. And you will be my kingdom of priests, my holy nation. This is the message you must give to the people of Israel.

SCRIPTURE
New Testament

Galations 3:26-28
For you are all children of God through faith in Christ Jesus. And all who have been united with Christ in baptism have put on Christ, like putting on new clothes. There is no longer Jew or Gentile, slave or free, male and female. For you are all one in Christ Jesus.

1. What is the Lord speaking into your life through these verses?

_____

_____

_____

2. What did you learn about the Lord?

_____

_____

Yesterday's Wins: _____

Yesterday's Challenges: _____

Lessons Learned: _____

_____

Today's Declaration: Today, I will...

_____

PRAYER
Today, I am praying for...

Who? _____ Why? _____

Who? _____ Why? _____

Who? _____ Why? _____

What? _____

What? _____

Praise: _____

Answered Prayers: _____

_____

_____

Let everyone try and find that as a result of daily prayer
he adds something new to his life,
something with which nothing can be compared.
-Mahatma Gandhi

> God loves each of us as if there were
> only one of us.
> -Augustine

ADDITIONAL THOUGHTS

_____

_____

_____

_____

_____

_____

_____

_____

_____

_____

_____

**WANT TO FILL YOUR DAY WITH
A CUP OF ENCOURAGEMENT?**
Experience the Weekday Podcast | _WeekdayPodcast.com_
5 minutes a day and 5 days a week
WeekdayPodcast.com

POWER ROUTINES _____ • _____ • _____   S   M   T   W   TH   F   S

GRATITUDE
Today, I am grateful for...

1. _____

2. _____

3. _____

When you are grateful for what you have, what you have is more than enough.

Proverbs 9:8-9
So don't bother correcting mockers; they will only hate you. But correct the wise, and they will love you. Instruct the wise, and they will be even wiser. Teach the righteous, and they will learn even more.

SCRIPTURE
Proverbs

Numbers 23:19-20
God is not a man, so he does not lie. He is not human, so he does not change his mind. Has he ever spoken and failed to act? Has he ever promised and not carried it through? Listen, I received a command to bless; God has blessed, and I cannot reverse it!

SCRIPTURE
Old Testament

Ephesians 1:3-4
All praise to God, the Father of our Lord Jesus Christ, who has blessed us with every spiritual blessing in the heavenly realms because we are united with Christ. Even before he made the world, God loved us and chose us in Christ to be holy and without fault in his eyes.

SCRIPTURE
New Testament

1. What is the Lord speaking into your life through these verses?

_____

_____

_____

2. What did you learn about the Lord?

_____

_____

Yesterday's Wins: _____

Yesterday's Challenges: _____

Lessons Learned: _____

_____

Today's Declaration: Today, I will...

_____

Who? _____   Why? _____

Who? _____   Why? _____

Who? _____   Why? _____

What? _____

What? _____

Praise: _____

Answered Prayers: _____

_____

_____

Prayer is the God-given communication
link between Heaven and Earth, time and
eternity, the finite and the infinite.
-Tony Evans

> You are the only Bible some
> unbelievers will ever read.
> -John MacArthur

_____

_____

_____

_____

_____

_____

_____

_____

_____

_____

Discover Peace, Power, & Direction
ON THE WEEKDAY MEDITATION
Meditative prayer guided by Pastor Chuck Allen
WeekdayMeditation.com

WEEKDAY
MEDITATION

GRATITUDE
Today, I am grateful for...

1. _____

2. _____

3. _____

When you are grateful for what you have, what you have is more than enough.

SCRIPTURE
Proverbs

Proverbs 9:11-12
Wisdom will multiply your days and add years to your life. If you become wise, you will be the one to benefit. If you scorn wisdom, you will be the one to suffer.

SCRIPTURE
Old Testament

Ecclesiastes 11:5-6
Just as you cannot understand the path of the wind or the mystery of a tiny baby growing in its mother's womb, so you cannot understand the activity of God, who does all things. Plant your seed in the morning and keep busy all afternoon, for you don't know if profit will come from one activity or another—or maybe both.

SCRIPTURE
New Testament

Ephesians 2:4-6
But God is so rich in mercy, and he loved us so much, that even though we were dead because of our sins, he gave us life when he raised Christ from the dead. For he raised us from the dead along with Christ and seated us with him in the heavenly realms because we are united with Christ Jesus.

1. What is the Lord speaking into your life through these verses?

_____

_____

_____

2. What did you learn about the Lord?

_____

_____

Yesterday's Wins: _____

Yesterday's Challenges: _____

Lessons Learned: _____

_____

Today's Declaration: Today, I will...

_____

PRAYER
Today, I am praying for...

Who? _____ Why? _____

Who? _____ Why? _____

Who? _____ Why? _____

What? _____

What? _____

Praise: _____

Answered Prayers: _____

_____

_____

The desire is thy prayers; and if thy desire is
without ceasing, thy prayer will also be without
ceasing. The continuance of your longing is the
continuance of your prayer.
-Saint Augustine

Continuous effort -- not strength nor
intelligence -- is the key to unlocking
our potential.
-Winston Churchill

_____

_____

_____

_____

_____

_____

_____

_____

_____

_____

**WANT TO FILL YOUR DAY WITH
A CUP OF ENCOURAGEMENT?**
Experience the Weekday Podcast | *WeekdayPodcast.com*
5 minutes a day and 5 days a week
WeekdayPodcast.com

POWER ROUTINES _____ • _____ • _____   S   M   T   W   TH   F   S

1. _____

2. _____

3. _____

When you are grateful for what you have, what you have is more than enough.

Proverbs 10:13-14
Wise words come from the lips of people with understanding, but those lacking sense will be beaten with a rod. Wise people treasure knowledge, but the babbling of a fool invites disaster.

SCRIPTURE
Proverbs

Jeremiah 1:6-8
"O Sovereign Lord," I said, "I can't speak for you! I'm too young!" The Lord replied, "Don't say, 'I'm too young,' for you must go wherever I send you and say whatever I tell you. And don't be afraid of the people, for I will be with you and will protect you. I, the Lord, have spoken!"

SCRIPTURE
Old Testament

Phillipians 2:3-5
Don't be selfish; don't try to impress others. Be humble, thinking of others as better than yourselves. Don't look out only for your own interests, but take an interest in others, too. You must have the same attitude that Christ Jesus had.

SCRIPTURE
New Testament

1. What is the Lord speaking into your life through these verses?

_____

_____

_____

2. What did you learn about the Lord?

_____

_____

Yesterday's Wins: _____

Yesterday's Challenges: _____

Lessons Learned: _____

_____

Today's Declaration: Today, I will...

_____

Who? _____   Why? _____

Who? _____   Why? _____

Who? _____   Why? _____

What? _____

What? _____

Praise: _____

Answered Prayers: _____

_____

_____

> ## Begin each day with private reading of the Word and prayer.
> ### -Jim Elliot

> We should live our lives as though Christ
> were coming this afternoon.
> -Jimmy Carter

ADDITIONAL THOUGHTS

_____

_____

_____

_____

_____

_____

_____

_____

_____

_____

_____

Discover Peace, Power, & Direction
ON THE WEEKDAY MEDITATION
Meditative prayer guided by Pastor Chuck Allen
WeekdayMeditation.com

WEEKDAY
MEDITATION

GRATITUDE
Today, I am grateful for...

1. _____

2. _____

3. _____

When you are grateful for what you have, what you have is more than enough.

SCRIPTURE
Proverbs

Proverbs 10:29-30
The way of the Lord is a stronghold to those with integrity, but it destroys the wicked. The godly will never be disturbed, but the wicked will be removed from the land.

SCRIPTURE
Old Testament

Joshua 1:7-8
Be strong and very courageous. Be careful to obey all the instructions Moses gave you. Do not deviate from them, turning either to the right or to the left. Then you will be successful in everything you do. Study this Book of Instruction continually. Meditate on it day and night so you will be sure to obey everything written in it. Only then will you prosper and succeed in all you do.

SCRIPTURE
New Testament

Colossians 2:6-7
And now, just as you accepted Christ Jesus as your Lord, you must continue to follow him. Let your roots grow down into him, and let your lives be built on him. Then your faith will grow strong in the truth you were taught, and you will overflow with thankfulness.

1. What is the Lord speaking into your life through these verses?

_____

_____

_____

2. What did you learn about the Lord?

_____

_____

Yesterday's Wins: _____

Yesterday's Challenges: _____

Lessons Learned: _____

_____

Today's Declaration: Today, I will...

_____

Who? _____ Why? _____

Who? _____ Why? _____

Who? _____ Why? _____

What? _____

What? _____

Praise: _____

Answered Prayers: _____

_____

_____

The soul is a muscle, and it needs to be exercised a
little every day. Say a morning prayer
just to say something.
-Catherine Hicks

> Choosing to be positive and having a
> grateful attitude is going to determine
> how you're going to live your life.
> -Joel Osteen

ADDITIONAL THOUGHTS

_____

_____

_____

_____

_____

_____

_____

_____

_____

_____

**WANT TO FILL YOUR DAY WITH
A CUP OF ENCOURAGEMENT?**
Experience the Weekday Podcast | *WeekdayPodcast.com*
5 minutes a day and 5 days a week
WeekdayPodcast.com

POWER ROUTINES _____ • _____ • _____   S   M   T   W   TH   F   S

Today, I am grateful for...

1. _____

2. _____

3. _____

When you are grateful for what you have, what you have is more than enough.

Proverbs 11:5-6
The way of the Lord is a stronghold to those with integrity, but it destroys the wicked. The godly will never be disturbed, but the wicked will be removed from the land. A wise youth harvests in the summer, but one who sleeps during harvest is a disgrace. The godly are showered with blessings; the words of the wicked conceal violent intentions.

SCRIPTURE
Proverbs

Isaiah 40:28-29
Have you never heard? Have you never understood? The Lord is the everlasting God, the Creator of all the earth. He never grows weak or weary. No one can measure the depths of his understanding. He gives power to the weak and strength to the powerless.

SCRIPTURE
Old Testament

1 Thessalonians 4:1-2
Finally, dear brothers and sisters, we urge you in the name of the Lord Jesus to live in a way that pleases God, as we have taught you. You live this way already, and we encourage you to do so even more. For you remember what we taught you by the authority of the Lord Jesus.

SCRIPTURE
New Testament

1. What is the Lord speaking into your life through these verses?

_____

_____

_____

2. What did you learn about the Lord?

_____

_____

Yesterday's Wins: _____

Yesterday's Challenges: _____

Lessons Learned: _____

_____

Today's Declaration: Today, I will...

_____

Who? _____   Why? _____

Who? _____   Why? _____

Who? _____   Why? _____

What? _____

What? _____

Praise: _____

Answered Prayers: _____

_____

_____

Prayer is where the action is.
-John Wesley

It doesn't matter what cards you're dealt. It's what you do with those cards. Never complain. Just keep pushing forward. Find a positive in anything and just fight for it.
-Baker Mayfield

ADDITIONAL THOUGHTS

_____

_____

_____

_____

_____

_____

_____

_____

_____

_____

Discover Peace, Power, & Direction
ON THE WEEKDAY MEDITATION
Meditative prayer guided by Pastor Chuck Allen
WeekdayMeditation.com

WEEKDAY
MEDITATION

POWER ROUTINES _____ • _____ • _____   S   M   T   W   TH   F   S

GRATITUDE
Today, I am grateful for...

1. _____

2. _____

3. _____

When you are grateful for what you have, what you have is more than enough.

SCRIPTURE
Proverbs

Proverbs 12:1-3
To learn, you must love discipline; it is stupid to hate correction. The Lord approves of those who are good, but he condemns those who plan wickedness. Wickedness never brings stability, but the godly have deep roots.

SCRIPTURE
Old Testament

Haggai 2:6-7
For this is what the Lord of Heaven's Armies says: In just a little while I will again shake the heavens and the earth, the oceans and the dry land. I will shake all the nations, and the treasures of all the nations will be brought to this Temple. I will fill this place with glory, says the Lord of Heaven's Armies. The silver is mine, and the gold is mine, says the Lord of Heaven's Armies.

SCRIPTURE
New Testament

Titus 2:7-8
And you yourself must be an example to them by doing good works of every kind. Let everything you do reflect the integrity and seriousness of your teaching. Teach the truth so that your teaching can't be criticized. Then those who oppose us will be ashamed and have nothing bad to say about us.

1. What is the Lord speaking into your life through these verses?

_____

_____

_____

2. What did you learn about the Lord?

_____

_____

Yesterday's Wins: _____

Yesterday's Challenges: _____

Lessons Learned: _____

_____

Today's Declaration: Today, I will...

_____

PRAYER
Today, I am praying for...

Who? _____ Why? _____

Who? _____ Why? _____

Who? _____ Why? _____

What? _____

What? _____

Praise: _____

Answered Prayers: _____

_____

_____

I pray to the God within me that He will give me
the strength to ask Him the right questions.
-Elie Wiesel

> I see possibilities in everything. For
> everything that's taken away, something
> of greater value has been given.
> -Michael J. Fox

ADDITIONAL THOUGHTS

_____

_____

_____

_____

_____

_____

_____

_____

_____

_____

THE WEEKDAY
PODCAST

WANT TO FILL YOUR DAY WITH
A CUP OF ENCOURAGEMENT?
Experience the Weekday Podcast | _WeekdayPodcast.com_
5 minutes a day and 5 days a week
WeekdayPodcast.com

POWER ROUTINES _____ • _____ • _____   S   M   T   W   TH   F   S

1. _____

2. _____

3. _____

When you are grateful for what you have, what you have is more than enough.

Proverbs 13:18-20
If you ignore criticism, you will end in poverty and disgrace; if you accept correction, you will be honored. It is pleasant to see dreams come true, but fools refuse to turn from evil to attain them. Walk with the wise and become wise; associate with fools and get in trouble.

SCRIPTURE
Proverbs

Isaiah 64:8-9
And yet, O Lord, you are our Father. We are the clay, and you are the potter. We all are formed by your hand. Don't be so angry with us, Lord. Please don't remember our sins forever. Look at us, we pray, and see that we are all your people.

SCRIPTURE
Old Testament

1 John 1:5-7
God is light, and there is no darkness in him at all. So we are lying if we say we have fellowship with God but go on living in spiritual darkness; we are not practicing the truth. But if we are living in the light, as God is in the light, then we have fellowship with each other, and the blood of Jesus, his Son, cleanses us.

SCRIPTURE
New Testament

1. What is the Lord speaking into your life through these verses?

_____

_____

_____

2. What did you learn about the Lord?

_____

_____

Yesterday's Wins: _____

Yesterday's Challenges: _____

Lessons Learned: _____

_____

Today's Declaration: Today, I will...

_____

PRAYER
Today, I am praying for...

Who? _____ Why? _____

Who? _____ Why? _____

Who? _____ Why? _____

What? _____

What? _____

Praise: _____

Answered Prayers: _____

_____

_____

> I find a great deal of comfort and care in
> my faith and prayer. I'd sooner
> do without air than prayer.
> -Mary Karr

> Success is not final, failure is not fatal: it is the courage to continue that counts.
> -Winston Churchill

ADDITIONAL THOUGHTS

_____

_____

_____

_____

_____

_____

_____

_____

_____

_____

Discover Peace, Power, & Direction
ON THE WEEKDAY MEDITATION
Meditative prayer guided by Pastor Chuck Allen
WeekdayMeditation.com

WEEKDAY
MEDITATION

GRATITUDE
Today, I am grateful for...

1. _____

2. _____

3. _____

When you are grateful for what you have, what you have is more than enough.

SCRIPTURE
Proverbs

Proverbs 16:2-3
People may be pure in their own eyes, but the Lord examines their motives. Commit your actions to the Lord , and your plans will succeed.

SCRIPTURE
Old Testament

2 Chronicles 20:29-30
When all the surrounding kingdoms heard that the Lord himself had fought against the enemies of Israel, the fear of God came over them. So Jehoshaphat's kingdom was at peace, for his God had given him rest on every side.

SCRIPTURE
New Testament

Romans 8:1-2
So now there is no condemnation for those who belong to Christ Jesus. And because you belong to him, the power of the life-giving Spirit has freed you from the power of sin that leads to death.

1. What is the Lord speaking into your life through these verses?

_____

_____

_____

2. What did you learn about the Lord?

_____

_____

Yesterday's Wins: _____

Yesterday's Challenges: _____

Lessons Learned: _____

_____

Today's Declaration: Today, I will...

_____

PRAYER
Today, I am praying for...

Who? _____ Why? _____

Who? _____ Why? _____

Who? _____ Why? _____

What? _____

What? _____

Praise: _____

Answered Prayers: _____

_____

_____

Prayer is the spirit speaking truth to Truth.
-Philip James Bailey

> There is nothing in this world that can
> compare with the Christian fellowship;
> nothing that can satisfy but Christ.
> -John D. Rockefeller

ADDITIONAL THOUGHTS

_____

_____

_____

_____

_____

_____

_____

_____

_____

_____

_____

**WANT TO FILL YOUR DAY WITH
A CUP OF ENCOURAGEMENT?**
Experience the Weekday Podcast | _WeekdayPodcast.com_
5 minutes a day and 5 days a week
WeekdayPodcast.com

POWER ROUTINES _____ • _____ • _____   S M T W TH F S

GRATITUDE
Today, I am grateful for...

1. _____

2. _____

3. _____

When you are grateful for what you have, what you have is more than enough.

SCRIPTURE
Proverbs

Proverbs 21:1-2
The king's heart is like a stream of water directed by the Lord; he guides it wherever he pleases. People may be right in their own eyes, but the Lord examines their heart.

SCRIPTURE
Old Testament

Job 1:20-22
Job stood up and tore his robe in grief. Then he shaved his head and fell to the ground to worship. He said, "I came naked from my mother's womb, and I will be naked when I leave. The Lord gave me what I had, and the Lord has taken it away. Praise the name of the Lord!" In all of this, Job did not sin by blaming God.

SCRIPTURE
New Testament

Mark 11:22-24
Have faith in God. I tell you the truth, you can say to this mountain, 'May you be lifted up and thrown into the sea,' and it will happen. But you must really believe it will happen and have no doubt in your heart. I tell you, you can pray for anything, and if you believe that you've received it, it will be yours.

1. What is the Lord speaking into your life through these verses?

_____

_____

_____

2. What did you learn about the Lord?

_____

_____

Yesterday's Wins: _____

Yesterday's Challenges: _____

Lessons Learned: _____

_____

Today's Declaration: Today, I will...

_____

PRAYER
Today, I am praying for...

Who? _____ Why? _____

Who? _____ Why? _____

Who? _____ Why? _____

What? _____

What? _____

Praise: _____

Answered Prayers: _____

_____

_____

Prayer should be the key of the day and the lock of the night.
-Thomas Fuller

> God is not asking you to be anything other than what he's made you, as long as you submit to how he has made you, to how you relate to other people who he has made different than you.
> -Tony Evans

_____

_____

_____

_____

_____

_____

_____

_____

_____

_____

Discover Peace, Power, & Direction
ON THE WEEKDAY MEDITATION
Meditative prayer guided by Pastor Chuck Allen
WeekdayMeditation.com

WEEKDAY
MEDITATION

POWER ROUTINES _____ • _____ • _____   S   M   T   W   TH   F   S

GRATITUDE
Today, I am grateful for...

1. _____

2. _____

3. _____

When you are grateful for what you have, what you have is more than enough.

SCRIPTURE
Proverbs

Proverbs 22:17-19
Listen to the words of the wise; apply your heart to my instruction. For it is good to keep these sayings in your heart and always ready on your lips. I am teaching you today—yes, you— so you will trust in the Lord.

SCRIPTURE
Old Testament

Job 42:1-3
Then Job replied to the Lord: "I know that you can do anything, and no one can stop you. You asked, 'Who is this that questions my wisdom with such ignorance?' It is I—and I was talking about things I knew nothing about, things far too wonderful for me."

SCRIPTURE
New Testament

Phillipians 3:10-11
I want to know Christ and experience the mighty power that raised him from the dead. I want to suffer with him, sharing in his death, so that one way or another I will experience the resurrection from the dead!

1. What is the Lord speaking into your life through these verses?

_____

_____

_____

2. What did you learn about the Lord?

_____

_____

Yesterday's Wins: _____

Yesterday's Challenges: _____

Lessons Learned: _____

_____

Today's Declaration: Today, I will...

_____

Who? _____ Why? _____

Who? _____ Why? _____

Who? _____ Why? _____

What? _____

What? _____

Praise: _____

Answered Prayers: _____

_____

_____

> To get nations back on their feet, we must
> first get down on our knees.
> -Billy Graham

> Never be afraid to trust an unknown
> future to a known God.
> -Corrie Ten Boom

ADDITIONAL THOUGHTS

_____

_____

_____

_____

_____

_____

_____

_____

_____

_____

**WANT TO FILL YOUR DAY WITH
A CUP OF ENCOURAGEMENT?**
Experience the Weekday Podcast | *WeekdayPodcast.com*
5 minutes a day and 5 days a week
WeekdayPodcast.com

1. _____

2. _____

3. _____

When you are grateful for what you have, what you have is more than enough.

Proverbs 23:4-5
Don't wear yourself out trying to get rich. Be wise enough to know when to quit. In the blink of an eye wealth disappears, for it will sprout wings and fly away like an eagle.

SCRIPTURE
Proverbs

Joel 2:12-13
That is why the Lord says, "Turn to me now, while there is time. Give me your hearts. Come with fasting, weeping, and mourning. Don't tear your clothing in your grief, but tear your hearts instead." Return to the Lord your God, for he is merciful and compassionate, slow to get angry and filled with unfailing love. He is eager to relent and not punish.

SCRIPTURE
Old Testament

2 Timothy 2:9-10
This is the Good News I preach. And because I preach this Good News, I am suffering and have been chained like a criminal. But the word of God cannot be chained. So I am willing to endure anything if it will bring salvation and eternal glory in Christ Jesus to those God has chosen.

SCRIPTURE
New Testament

1. What is the Lord speaking into your life through these verses?

_____

_____

_____

2. What did you learn about the Lord?

_____

_____

Yesterday's Wins: _____

Yesterday's Challenges: _____

Lessons Learned: _____

_____

Today's Declaration: Today, I will...

_____

PRAYER
Today, I am praying for...

Who? _____ Why? _____

Who? _____ Why? _____

Who? _____ Why? _____

What? _____

What? _____

Praise: _____

Answered Prayers: _____

_____

_____

Prayer is talking with God. God knows your
heart and is not so concerned with your words
as He is with the attitude of your heart.
-Josh McDowell

> Finish each day and be done with it. You have done what you could. Some blunders and absurdities no doubt crept in; forget them as soon as you can. Tomorrow is a new day.
> -Ralph Waldo Emerson

ADDITIONAL THOUGHTS

_____

_____

_____

_____

_____

_____

_____

_____

_____

_____

Discover Peace, Power, & Direction
ON THE WEEKDAY MEDITATION
Meditative prayer guided by Pastor Chuck Allen
WeekdayMeditation.com

WEEKDAY
MEDITATION

POWER ROUTINES _____ • _____ • _____   S M T W TH F S

GRATITUDE
Today, I am grateful for...

1. _____

2. _____

3. _____

When you are grateful for what you have, what you have is more than enough.

SCRIPTURE
Proverbs

Proverbs 24:1-2
Don't envy evil people or desire their company. For their hearts plot violence, and their words always stir up trouble.

SCRIPTURE
Old Testament

Jonah 2:5-7
I sank beneath the waves, and the waters closed over me. Seaweed wrapped itself around my head. I sank down to the very roots of the mountains. I was imprisoned in the earth, whose gates lock shut forever. But you, O Lord my God, snatched me from the jaws of death! As my life was slipping away, I remembered the Lord.

SCRIPTURE
New Testament

2 Thessalonians 2:16-17
Now may our Lord Jesus Christ himself and God our Father, who loved us and by his grace gave us eternal comfort and a wonderful hope, comfort you and strengthen you in every good thing you do and say.

1. What is the Lord speaking into your life through these verses?

_____

_____

_____

2. What did you learn about the Lord?

_____

_____

Yesterday's Wins: _____

Yesterday's Challenges: _____

Lessons Learned: _____

_____

Today's Declaration: Today, I will...

_____

PRAYER
Today, I am praying for...

Who? _____ Why? _____

Who? _____ Why? _____

Who? _____ Why? _____

What? _____

What? _____

Praise: _____

Answered Prayers: _____

_____

_____

Prayer, the word of God, and His Spirit should be united
together. We should go to the Lord repeatedly in prayer,
and ask Him to teach us by His Spirit through His word.
-George Muller

> Once we believe in ourselves, we can risk curiosity, wonder, spontaneous delight, or any experience that reveals the human spirit.
> -E. E. Cummings

ADDITIONAL THOUGHTS

_____

_____

_____

_____

_____

_____

_____

_____

_____

_____

**WANT TO FILL YOUR DAY WITH
A CUP OF ENCOURAGEMENT?**
Experience the Weekday Podcast | *WeekdayPodcast.com*
5 minutes a day and 5 days a week
WeekdayPodcast.com

POWER ROUTINES _____ • _____ • _____   S   M   T   W   TH   F   S

1. _____

2. _____

3. _____

When you are grateful for what you have, what you have is more than enough.

Proverbs 24:17-18
Don't rejoice when your enemies fall; don't be happy when they stumble. For the Lord will be displeased with you and will turn his anger away from them.

SCRIPTURE
Proverbs

Nehimiah 1:5-7
O Lord, God of heaven, the great and awesome God who keeps his covenant of unfailing love with those who love him and obey his commands, listen to my prayer! Look down and see me praying night and day for your people Israel. I confess that we have sinned against you. Yes, even my own family and I have sinned!

SCRIPTURE
Old Testament

Mark 16:5-6
When they entered the tomb, they saw a young man clothed in a white robe sitting on the right side. The women were shocked, but the angel said, "Don't be alarmed. You are looking for Jesus of Nazareth, who was crucified. He isn't here! He is risen from the dead! Look, this is where they laid his body."

SCRIPTURE
New Testament

1. What is the Lord speaking into your life through these verses?

_____

_____

_____

2. What did you learn about the Lord?

_____

_____

Yesterday's Wins: _____

Yesterday's Challenges: _____

Lessons Learned: _____

_____

Today's Declaration: Today, I will...

_____

Who? _____ Why? _____

Who? _____ Why? _____

Who? _____ Why? _____

What? _____

What? _____

Praise: _____

Answered Prayers: _____

_____

_____

Let us never forget to pray. God lives. He is near. He is
real. He is not only aware of us but cares for us. He is
our Father. He is accessible to all who will seek Him.
-Gordon B. Hinckley

> Life is wasted if we do not grasp the glory of the cross, cherish it for the treasure that it is, and cleave to it as the highest price of every pleasure and the deepest comfort in every pain.
> -John Piper

ADDITIONAL THOUGHTS

Discover Peace, Power, & Direction
ON THE WEEKDAY MEDITATION
Meditative prayer guided by Pastor Chuck Allen
WeekdayMeditation.com

WEEKDAY
MEDITATION

POWER ROUTINES _____ • _____ • _____   S M T W TH F S

GRATITUDE
Today, I am grateful for...

1. _____

2. _____

3. _____

When you are grateful for what you have, what you have is more than enough.

SCRIPTURE
Proverbs

Proverbs 25:21-22
*If your enemies are hungry, give them food to eat.
If they are thirsty, give them water to drink. You will
heap burning coals of shame on their heads, and the
Lord will reward you.*

SCRIPTURE
Old Testament

2 Chronicles 7:14-15
*Then if my people who are called by my name will
humble themselves and pray and seek my face and
turn from their wicked ways, I will hear from heaven
and will forgive their sins and restore their land. My
eyes will be open and my ears attentive to every
prayer made in this place.*

SCRIPTURE
New Testament

James 1:2-4
*Dear brothers and sisters, when troubles of any kind
come your way, consider it an opportunity for great
joy. For you know that when your faith is tested, your
endurance has a chance to grow. So let it grow, for
when your endurance is fully developed, you will be
perfect and complete, needing nothing.*

1. What is the Lord speaking into your life through these verses?

_____

_____

_____

2. What did you learn about the Lord?

_____

_____

Yesterday's Wins: _____

Yesterday's Challenges: _____

Lessons Learned: _____

_____

Today's Declaration: Today, I will...

_____

PRAYER
Today, I am praying for...

Who? _____   Why? _____

Who? _____   Why? _____

Who? _____   Why? _____

What? _____

What? _____

Praise: _____

Answered Prayers: _____

_____

_____

In prayer it is better to have a heart without
words than words without a heart.
-John Bunyan

> The one who obeys God's instruction for today will develop a keen awareness of His direction for tomorrow.
> -Lysa Terkeurst

ADDITIONAL THOUGHTS

_____
_____
_____
_____
_____
_____
_____
_____
_____
_____
_____

THE WEEKDAY
PODCAST

**WANT TO FILL YOUR DAY WITH
A CUP OF ENCOURAGEMENT?**
Experience the Weekday Podcast | *WeekdayPodcast.com*
5 minutes a day and 5 days a week
WeekdayPodcast.com

GRATITUDE
Today, I am grateful for...

1. _____

2. _____

3. _____

When you are grateful for what you have, what you have is more than enough.

Proverbs 26:4-5
*Don't answer the foolish arguments of fools, or you
will become as foolish as they are. Be sure to answer
the foolish arguments of fools, or they will become
wise in their own estimation.*

SCRIPTURE
Proverbs

Numbers 14:8-9
*And if the Lord is pleased with us, he will bring us
safely into that land and give it to us. It is a rich land
flowing with milk and honey. Do not rebel against the
Lord , and don't be afraid of the people of the land.
They are only helpless prey to us! They have no
protection, but the Lord is with us! Don't be afraid of
them!*

SCRIPTURE
Old Testament

1 Peter 1:6-7
*There is wonderful joy ahead, even though you must
endure many trials for a little while. These trials will
show that your faith is genuine. It is being tested as
fire tests and purifies gold—though your faith is far
more precious than mere gold.*

SCRIPTURE
New Testament

1. What is the Lord speaking into your life through these verses?

_____

_____

_____

2. What did you learn about the Lord?

_____

_____

Yesterday's Wins: _____

Yesterday's Challenges: _____

Lessons Learned: _____

_____

Today's Declaration: Today, I will...

_____

Who? _____   Why? _____

Who? _____   Why? _____

Who? _____   Why? _____

What? _____

What? _____

Praise: _____

Answered Prayers: _____

_____

_____

Do not pray for easy lives. Pray to be stronger men.
-John F. Kennedy

Are you worrying about something God has
already worked out?
-Steven Furtick

ADDITIONAL THOUGHTS

_____

_____

_____

_____

_____

_____

_____

_____

_____

_____

_____

Discover Peace, Power, & Direction
ON THE WEEKDAY MEDITATION
Meditative prayer guided by Pastor Chuck Allen
WeekdayMeditation.com

WEEKDAY
MEDITATION

GRATITUDE
Today, I am grateful for...

1. _____

2. _____

3. _____

When you are grateful for what you have, what you have is more than enough.

SCRIPTURE
Proverbs

Proverbs 27:9-10
The heartfelt counsel of a friend is as sweet as perfume and incense. Never abandon a friend— either yours or your father's. When disaster strikes, you won't have to ask your brother for assistance. It's better to go to a neighbor than to a brother who lives far away.

SCRIPTURE
Old Testament

Lamentations 3:37-39
Who can command things to happen without the Lord's permission? Does not the Most High send both calamity and good? Then why should we, mere humans, complain when we are punished for our sins?

SCRIPTURE
New Testament

Jude 1:20-21
But you, dear friends, must build each other up in your most holy faith, pray in the power of the Holy Spirit, and await the mercy of our Lord Jesus Christ, who will bring you eternal life. In this way, you will keep yourselves safe in God's love.

1. What is the Lord speaking into your life through these verses?

_____

_____

_____

2. What did you learn about the Lord?

_____

_____

Yesterday's Wins: _____

Yesterday's Challenges: _____

Lessons Learned: _____

_____

Today's Declaration: Today, I will...

_____

PRAYER
Today, I am praying for...

Who? _____ Why? _____

Who? _____ Why? _____

Who? _____ Why? _____

What? _____

What? _____

Praise: _____

Answered Prayers: _____

_____

_____

Don't forget to pray today because God did not forget to wake you up this morning.
-Oswald Chambers

> And my God will supply every need of yours
> according to his riches in glory
> in Christ Jesus.
> -Phillipians 4:19

ADDITIONAL THOUGHTS

_____

_____

_____

_____

_____

_____

_____

_____

_____

_____

**WANT TO FILL YOUR DAY WITH
A CUP OF ENCOURAGEMENT?**
Experience the Weekday Podcast | *WeekdayPodcast.com*
5 minutes a day and 5 days a week
WeekdayPodcast.com

POWER ROUTINES _____ • _____ • _____   S M T W TH F S

1. _____

2. _____

3. _____

When you are grateful for what you have, what you have is more than enough.

Proverbs 30:5-6
Evil people don't understand justice, but those who follow the Lord understand completely. Better to be poor and honest than to be dishonest and rich.

SCRIPTURE
Proverbs

Psalm 27:11-13
Teach me how to live, O Lord . Lead me along the right path, for my enemies are waiting for me. Do not let me fall into their hands. For they accuse me of things I've never done; with every breath they threaten me with violence. Yet I am confident I will see the Lord's goodness while I am here in the land of the living.

SCRIPTURE
Old Testament

Hebrews 9:11-12
So Christ has now become the High Priest over all the good things that have come. He has entered that greater, more perfect Tabernacle in heaven, which was not made by human hands... With his own blood... he entered the Most Holy Place once for all time and secured our redemption forever.

SCRIPTURE
New Testament

1. What is the Lord speaking into your life through these verses?

_____

_____

_____

2. What did you learn about the Lord?

_____

_____

Yesterday's Wins: _____

Yesterday's Challenges: _____

Lessons Learned: _____

_____

Today's Declaration: Today, I will...

_____

PRAYER
Today, I am praying for...

Who? _____ Why? _____

Who? _____ Why? _____

Who? _____ Why? _____

What? _____

What? _____

Praise: _____

Answered Prayers: _____

_____

_____

Prayer at its highest is a two-way conversation-and
for me the most important part is
listening to God's replies.
-Frank C. Laubach

> Your time is limited, so don't waste it living someone else's life. And most important, have the courage to follow your heart and intuition.
> -Steve Jobs

ADDITIONAL THOUGHTS

_____

_____

_____

_____

_____

_____

_____

_____

_____

_____

_____

Discover Peace, Power, & Direction
ON THE WEEKDAY MEDITATION
Meditative prayer guided by Pastor Chuck Allen
WeekdayMeditation.com

WEEKDAY
MEDITATION